Pray... Don't Faint... Believe

by

Tracy Ferguson Cooper

Pray… Don't Faint… Believe

Copyright © 2021 by (Tracy Ferguson Cooper)

All rights reserved. No part of this book may be reproduced or transmitted in any form or by any means without written permission from the author.

Published by:
Ware Resources and Publishing
www.wareresources.com

1-888-469-4850 Ext. 2

ISBN (978-1-736-0798-3-6)
LCCN: 2021906089

Printed in USA by Ware Resources and Publishing

Auto Graph Page

Table of Contents

A Friend	7
Black Heroes	8
Just Speaking	10
Don't You Have Anything To Say	11
The Number Is Six	13
No Greater Love	15
To Be Loved	16
Nobody Knows	17
So Nice	19
Your Gift	21
Juneteenth	22
A Minute	24
Watch To See	25
Run To God	27
Come Back	28
No One	30
God Cares For You	31
X Marks The Spot	32
Make Someone's Day	33
Know Someone	34

A Listening God	35
This Is Not Over	36
We Are Not Out Own	38
But God	39
There Is A God	40
An Open Shame	41
Saving Us	42
Your Body	44
God Is With You	45
Mom's Prayers	46
Go Be Great	47
Easy Love	49
You Win	50
Take It Slow	52
Dysfunction	53
Relationship	54
Pray… Don't Faint… Believe	55
Go With God	56
Lost And, Turned Out	58
They Go On	60
Are You Really For This	62
I Still Love You	64

Clothe Yourself …………………………………..	65
Dark Skin ………………………………………	66
I Miss You ………………………………………	67
Fixed ……………………………………………	69
Angry Son ………………………………………	70
This Simple Thing ………………………………	72
Separate ……………………………………….	74
I Love You ………………………………………	76
No More Mask …………………………………	79
About the Author --------------------------------	81

About The Author

Tracy Ferguson Cooper, a graduate of The University of Delaware, developed an affinity for writing poetry at the age of 12 which has lasted until this very day... Mr. Cooper has written three books of poetry: Seas... Sands.... Poems... Pictures (2012 in collaboration with photographer Paul Romangoli) Grace And Mercy (2019-Liberations Publishing) Pray... Don't Faint... Believe (2021) Mr. Cooper has received a grant toward the publication of Pray... Don't Faint... Believe.

This collection open poetry and prose stems from what we have seen played out in the media... A reflection of what black and brown people's have struggled with in their quest for basic equal rights... It is also an inspirational book of encouragement giving hope... And also it is a history lesson which depicts black and brown persons as auspicious and enterprising.

It is believed that the reader (no matter what color or nationality) will be educated and enlightened... uplifted... motivated... It is my hope that anyone who reads each piece of poetry and prose contained within the pages will be made better... This collection is inspirational and informational.

And now
You exercise
Erroneous privilege
We won't tolerate it any longer
It's a miscarriage of justice
A system in place
We can't embrace
There's a shift
To uplift
To our rightful place
No more masks

A Friend

I have an everlasting companion
With me until the very end
I'm never abandoned
He isn't fake
He doesn't pretend
To care
He is always fair
Never leaving nor forsaking
Always the time taking
Perfecting all concerning
He has no shadow of turning
From me
I take comfort in knowing
He always hears me
My prayers
Even if they are tears
No matter how much I suffer
Or prosper
In either case I have peace
I know deep in my soul
His faithfulness I behold
I'm fortunate enough to know
Closer than a brother
I've Got a Friend

Painters and sculptors
Doctors and lawyers
Bankers and engineers
Teachers and nurses
So many more to mention
Who had and have the intention
To be the best they ever could be
Meaningful and legendary
They are super
Black Heroes

Black Heroes

So much information
Has been hidden
For so long
For Generations
Centuries
Triumphs
And pleasantries
Of Kingdoms
So prosperous
In Africa
And settlers
Here before pilgrims
And Columbus
They were indigenous
In America
Unbeknownst to so many of us
Lost somehow
In the history books
Is how some prospered
Cowboys
Frontiersman
Oh yes… amen
Many contributions
Inventors
And builders
The talented tenth
Holders and makers
Movers and shakers
Chain breakers
Making a mark
Impact
Singers and musicians
Dancers and actors
Directors and producers

Don't You Have Anything To Say

For or against
Yay or nay
What do you say
Don't be shy
On the fence
Of your stance
Can one be convinced
In these times uncertain
For you what is or isn't working
You have a dog in the fight
Skin in the game
About what's going down
Let it rain
A position maintain
Do not refrain
Upon what do you frown
What do you think is insane
Important or good
Don't you care to shed any light
Are you passionate
Do you just want to be understood
You don't have to be polite
If angry you should let it be known
You don't have to sin
What are you feeling
How are you dealing
Don't be mute
Please air your concerns
And frustrations
Or pleasantries
Simply do not remain
Safe and quiet
Utter a sound
Your opinion counts

Just Speaking

When you sit in a room
With a family member
Have the courtesy please
To speak a simple hello
It could make their day
When in the company
Of an idle stranger
Utter a love language
It could relieve any anguish
They may be feeling
A simple act of kindness
Let all of creation
In you find this
While in your midst
For you never know
When you are entertaining
Angels from on high
Be that girl or guy
Give love a try
By just speaking

The Number Is Six

The number is six
That I have heard
That have perished
Mainly unjustly
The number
Remains fixed
In our souls
Because cherished
Were these lives
That God gave
Family and friends
The opportunity to behold
Now these six
As a nation
We mourn
They were taken
Much too soon
Our hearts are aching
It's an old familiar tune
That the lives of black and brown skin
Don't count at all
But I say to you
They are beautiful
And by all means
God chosen
But lives
You have stolen
Whether
Procedure took place
Or premeditated
It's a horror and disgrace
Did you mean to kill
Because you could
Did you think

It can speak volumes
Be no longer silent
Don't you have anything to say

No Greater Love

There is none more pure
That can be desired
That is worth living for
Surely none is more true
Making a sacrifice
Paying an awful price
Going through an ugly ordeal
Helpless… Selfless
Determined… Devoted
Absolutely divine
Having compassion so fine
Giving his life for yours and mine
There's no greater love

That those six
That were black and brown
Should not be around
Were just no good
Who are you to decide
Malice played a part
You fired or choked
You silenced potential
These six
Are no more
These six
Should have endured
But they could not breathe
Prematurely they had to leave
These six
How many more

To Be Loved

Touching someone's soul
Can be more precious than gold
Reaching them on the inside
Making them thrive
Can extraordinarily revive
Their spirit energize
Kindness and affection
Making them rise
Deliver untouched them this prize
Yet while they can behold
To your goodness let them be exposed
Compassion release
Genuinely let it show
Uplift the hurting
They are deserving of tenderness
So when you have a chance
Take it upon yourself to bless
They will appreciate it
Cause as far as they're concerned
Nothing else can compare
Nothing is as special
Than to be loved

Nobody Knows

Some in this world are needful
They want for love and acceptance
Truth is…. They are hurting and thundering for compassion
For so long they've been mistreated and neglected
In the heart more than we will ever know
If no one reaches out they remain adversely affected
So they inflict pain to others
Unsuspecting victims
Until they suffer
Or even death kicks in
To those care show
Love conquers all
God is love
You reap what you sow
Plainly to every man
Love we owe
Through something
We all go
Some lesser
But some greater
Instead of lovers
They become haters
They feel a certain way
Cause theirs is a cry for help
Kind affection show
Listen
Pray
Faithfulness to them show
Love on them
Nobody Knows
What intentions they have
Maybe we can change perspective
Whatever experience that they have had
Nobody Knows

Love conquers all
Nobody Knows

So Nice

It's a great knowing
A new day to us
God is showing
His mercy and grace
Is still flowing
Like a river
Or even an ocean deep
Into us He let
The breath of life
Once more speak
Once more He gave us
One more day
His face to seek
Giving us direction
To navigate
This wicked world
Guiding our steps
In a plain path
So very correct
For what comes next
Leading us into
The way we should go
When we are on one accord
Making the proper connection
So we are on board
Within God's will
Without exception
He is faithful
To one and all
He is truly able
To keep us
Not letting us fall
Shower the Almighty
With continual praise

Who paid our price
Love on the Most High
Who left us His spirit
To be our guide
We could very well
Take it for granted
It is so nice
Thank you Lord
Hallelujah

Your Gift

You have been blessed
With certain gifts
And abilities
Don't hide them
Use them
Serve with them
Your Gift extend
Whether it be
Hospitality
Or comedy
Writing
Speaking
Reciting poetry
If you are inclined
Musically
Your Gift
Was intended
By God
To be shared
Not spared
So shine
With your talent
God given
Don't let it be hidden
These precious gems
Expose these
Engage
Amaze
On the stage
Or one on one
Our senses captivated
Let them be appreciated
So very elevated
Your Gift

Juneteenth

A celebration
A revelation
Fulfillment
Of a dream
A thing
Surreal
Just the idea
So extreme
To be free
From bondage
Physically
And mentally
To toil no more
What they endured
Separation of family
Rape of our women
Castration of our men
What outright humiliation
A tragedy plainly
They could now rejoice
They could lift their voice
Thanking God
Perhaps shedding a tear
Oh so happy
So many years
They wept
So painstakingly
Thinking this day
They would never see
Let us commemorate
Exuberantly
Excellently
This monumental time
In history

A thing of beauty
Juneteenth

A Minute

Hear the Holy Spirit
To lead you on your way
On the straight and narrow road
Otherwise it could be finished
On the wide and spacious way
Trust and obey
Let God have His way
Where there's no limits
Don't cater to self
In order to get wealth
When the Lord
Is all the help
You'll ever need
Look to Him
Look to win
In everyday life
It will never be diminished
In a minute

Watch To See

Some on social media
That you see
When you look
A thing of beauty
They appear to be
But some more on the mission
They may indeed catch fish
They have one desire
Only one wish
To take advantage
To wipe you out
To scam
There is no doubt
You are a target
The bomb goes off
Bam
They have cheated
Robbed and swindled
Making dollars dwindled
You are humiliated
Embarrassed
To say the least
But they rejoice
Pulling off the caper
Looking so good so sweet
Doing evil
Having your paper
You had no hunch
You were unsuspecting
No clue
To be safer
Cuts like a knife
Stings like a teaser
A lesson learned

They looked so good
But you hurt so bad
Making you burned
Leaving you empty
Your pockets
It's a shock
And undeserved
You're perturbed
At yourself
Placing blame on you
But you can't believe
Everything
On social media
To be true
Watch to see

Run To God

Be careful
Stay prayerful
Don't neglect
Your first love
Make haste
Cause the Lion out there
In the streets
Is seeking
Who he may devour
This very moment
And alone in your power
You can never combat him
Satan the devil
Is on another level
And wants your soul
You must not relinquish control
Go with God for He is truly good
Almighty
The only wise God
Victorious
Holy and Glorious
A Strong Tower
To run to when there's trouble
You can be safe
The evil one wants your soul
But you must stay whole
Daily make it your goal
To run to God

Come Back

Sometimes
I fall short
I'm not of a good report
Yes I do find
The will and way
On the straight and narrow road
I abort
I'm sorry to say
This path I would not recommend
Having to start over and repent
While all the time
I should have maintained
A made up mind
I have been lost
Cause I didn't seek His face
And my life held no promise
I have longed after carnal pleasures
Really an empty waste
Leaving me only in an empty space
But God has never given up on me
He has with open arms
Once again accepted me
Welcoming me home
It's a clean slate
But please I urge you
Don't let God have to purge you
When you don't have to
Practice His presence
Daily on one accord
Moving forward
Living in the last days
Having the wherewithal
And the knack
When you fall

To realize your mistakes
And come back

No One

Know God
Become
Holy and tender
Precious
In His eyesight
Show God
Surrender
To the power
Of His might
Flow with God
Endeavor
To walk worthy
In His light
Grow with God
Let Him not be
Disregarded
Doing His will
Being a great delight
Glow with God
As your soul shines
Through His countenance
Follow God
Stand in God
Go with God
For He alone
Is good
No one is like the Lord
No one in the universe
Who is like the Lord
No one
The only one
God

God Cares For You

If God cares for the sparrows
Then how much more
Does He care for you
You are precious
In His sight
Walk in His way
A light guiding
Definitely true
Faithful
He will prove
Never leaving nor forsaking you
He makes a way from none for you
Jesus died for me and you
His one and only son
Forgiving our sins
Paying our price
Selflessly
God Cares for you

X Marks The Spot

If I am a black man
In America
Am I a target
If alone on a dark lit street
Do I have to fear for my life
I am innocent
But will there be a violation
Of my human rights
Even if I am complicit
Not putting up a fight
Not resisting
But body blows
Will they be inflicting
Upon my frame
Brutality
Will they do just more of the same
And not be blamed
Not found guilty
Continue their wicked reign
Rogue cops
X Marks the spot

Make Someone's Day

So many go without
Day in and Day out
Struggling to make it
But bread you break it
Help widows and orphans
Goodwill extend
The moment apprehend
Opportunities abound
Just look around
Homelessness is epidemic
Not to bless
The less fortunate
Having little to nothing
Do something
It's okay to pray
Do good also in deed
A little child feed
Bless a family
Suffering calamity
Don't turn and walk away
In you let God have His way
Make someone's day

Know Someone

Get to know someone
Before you count them out
Or upon their character
Exercise judgment
Don't be the very one
Trying to create doubt
It isn't fair
Without even making an acquaintance
You didn't even get to sample
Their true essence
From a perceived image
Through media Outlets
With them you're just finished
You have made them diminished
In your mind
Without knowing someone
They are not as fine
God made them
They are precious in His sight
O woe unto you
There is pay back
From the Divine
Just because you
Thought you were too far above someone
Exercising prejudice and stereotypes
Not at all are you that fine
Before really knowing someone

A Listening God

Our prayers
God hears
He cares
And won't turn a deaf ear
Every word He heeds
No shadow of turning
Our most desperate plea
According to His will to trust
Every tear He also captures
Acknowledging their silence
For they are genuine
And not manufactured
There is no defiance
You must have faith
Simply believe
On God with integrity wait
That He will meet our needs
Because He is able
And so good
A listening God

This Is Not Over

Plain as can be
So very pointed
Every protest and rally
They won't be turned away
Not disappointed
Until heard
For the damage done
From the bondage
Wrongdoing of so many of a one
They will not look beyond it
Until served
For centuries now
Second-class citizenship
Endurance upheld somehow
But you still tighten your grip
The gruesome pot stirred
Oh no this will not diminish
The hunger of the cause will only intensify
They will march with determined footsteps
You murdered... Too many of us had to die
Too much regret... Gone too soon
They are too very disturbed
So many have gathered before
And not completely in vain
Martin and others endured
But only for a short season was there change
What lately has occurred
But the brutality of the Mississippi cotton fields
Where unbearable toil took place
If there was a work stoppage even momentarily
The whip ensued
Cries were uttered
Moving forward present day
Homicides in a month's time

A half dozen or so
Happening every day
Unnecessarily so
In Baltimore
Remember Freddie Gray
Remember all the tragedies
Including the latest
The George Floyd death by knee
He was not resisting
And for a bounced check
The rogue cop pressed down
With just enough pressure upon his neck
To kill him dead
Just another example a blatant disregard of
Black and brown people
Suffering evil
Not considered equal
So this is fuel to their fire
Protesters are now inspired
And by no means
Will there be any let up
This is not over

We Are Not Out Own

This body a soul
Is made for service
Tame this body
Under control
Let it's stirrings be devoted
Reaching out
In service
Reasonable
With spirit agreeable
Cast no doubt
Let not your good
Be not evil spoken of
Be wise as a serpent
But as gentle as a dove
Watch
Pray
Be purposed by design
As to love
You're well inclined
Everyday
On purpose
In a zone
Owe no man
Nothing but love
We are commanded to do this
We are not our own

But God

There is nothing to say to me but God
There's nothing to do about it but believe
Have faith and pray
God is not finished with me yet
This fate I don't accept
Because He has my times in His hands
And for me He has so many plans
So I am determined
In His will to stand
So His will
I will fulfill
What else can I do
But watch the Almighty move
Faithful He will prove
But God

There Is A God

So many mock and scorn
And their conduct is flawed
They fail to see the truth
The Almighty they reverence not
They decide even that the Most High
Does not exist
Oh how foolish are these
Who are mere men
Who continue in their sin
When their end comes
It is really a beginning
Doom and despair
For iniquity
And unbelief
Their penalty
For being obstinate
Stiff necked
They will pay
Lost in their own way
They choose to disobey
They didn't realize
Only He
Is the truth life and way
Finally they will expire
Without acknowledging
There Is A God

An Open Shame

Tired of this
I could not resist
Once more the mark I missed
Satan right in the mouth if I kissed
Left feeling illegitimate
Having to repent
I need to quit
Bring it to an end
So I can really represent
Let my little light shine
So they can see you so fine
I must crucify my flesh
Instead of being an awful mess
I kept going back to it
Over and over again
I couldn't see it wasn't worth it
Please oh Lord
Take this desire from within
Free me from this iniquity
Set me on the path to being on one accord
Release me from this needless pain
With my mouth I repent
In my heart I now abstain
For putting you Lord
To an open shame

Saving Us

Why can't all of us live
We must stop all this killing
Black on black
In a sea of red
Should leave us feeling
A shade of midnight blue
Please consider
That any life you take
Any crushing blow
You deliver
Has been created by God
And wasn't meant
To prematurely and unjustifiably go
You will have to give
Your answers
To the ultimate God
For the taking of a soul
Perhaps innocent
Or not at all
Black people as a race
By so many whites
Have been debased
So why give place
To evil the same
It is obviously plain
These homicides
Make a hideous stain
Leaving enormous pain
Why must we be crying
For the lost of our very own
So many dying
At our hands
Yes for our sins we must atone
We are applying a choke hold

We are to an extent unjust
A segment of unruly culprits
That won't quit
We must go about
Make it a mission to love us
No longer mistreat us
Defeat us
We must make more of an effort
Of saving us

Your Body

A temple
Sacred
An example
Divine
Handcrafted
By the Almighty
Dwelling
Where
Jesus is
Spiritually
This house
Maintain
From Overdoing it
Abstain
For its creation
Is beautiful
And pure
Cherish
Your being
Don't take it
For granted
A gift from God
A masterpiece
Excellent
In its form
Your body

God Is With You

Plead the blood of Jesus
Decree and declare
The word of God
In the atmosphere
Do not be intimidated
Fight the good fight of faith
For our God is able
And faithful
And undefeated
You are the healed
You are the saved
Believe you win
Make sure you aren't cheated
Exercise your authority
In the Lord's ability
 No weapon against you prospers
Do not falter
Leave it at the altar
Never fear
El Shadai
Is present more than enough
Total source of your supply
Be confident in the God
Who is first and last
Who cannot be surpassed
All powerful
Almighty
Do not be afraid
God is with you

Mom's Prayers

I hardly spent any time
Properly with you
A bond wasn't formed
I knew I was your last born
At the age of almost fourty
Back then being pregnant
Was not something you'd do
Thank you for loving me enough
For letting me come to fruition
Even though I was sickly
You never gave up on me
And now I see
All this time
You were my advocate
A voice in Heaven
Speaking on my behalf
When I had no strength
To last
You asked
God
To stop
The devil
In this tracks
God heard you
A breakthrough
Occurred
With mom's prayers

Go Be Great

You were born
No just for the sake
Of being born
You are here
On this earth
To be somebody special
You are divinely pre-ordained
You have God given purpose
For such a time as this
If you stay focused on God
Yeah if you don't resist
Your calling
The life you are living
The chance
You've been given
Will not be in vain
It will have some difficulty
But remember
You were built for this
So train and work
And study
So you are not ill equipped
On this stay fixed
To fulfil destiny
Your season
Has reason
You were blessed to be
Somebody
Unique and driven
So go on and be a light
Yes so brightly shine
Giving someone else hope
You were born
To not be ordinary

No... You were born
To be epic
Purposed by design
As mountains you climb
To the top
And conquer
Being extraordinary
You were born
To touch somebody's life
Always giving Glory to God
For your talent and ability
So now go carve out
 your niche in history
Knowing you were meant for
 all of this
So stay focused
Stay fixed
On the prize
Rise
Accelerate
Speaking faith
Demonstrate
Elevate
You were born
So spread your wings
In this moment
Yes... Go be great

Easy Love

You've been searching
For a love
Unrequited
And real
Who gets you
Who gets through
To your heart
Having appeal
Not trying to tear it apart
But instead build it up
Making harmony
Not willing to disrupt
But love is a work in progress
It surely isn't automatic
You must give it your all
You must be emphatic
Be romantic
And understanding
Never abandon
Nor take for granted
Their feelings
Revealing
A generous and devoted soul
In order to make your relationship whole
Fulfilling that role
Of a great mate
Putting God first
Giving this a chance to work
An Easy Love

You Win

Sometimes
It's unavoidable
It can't be helped
It comes upon you
And lingers
Holding on
If not prayed up
On your own
In your flesh
It is of no use
To combat it
Not enough
Depression
If not careful
Will take up
Residence
And whisper
You're worthless
Give up
But for you
This doesn't haven't to be true
You can survive
While going through
A way of escape exist
As this demonic onslaught
You resist
As you respond
Calling on the name of Jesus
Lord of Lords
King of Kings
Say that name
The name that is named
Over every thing
That is named

You can thrive
As you abide
In the presence
Of the Almighty
An essence
That speaks
Victory
Yielding no ground
And greatly abounds
Where you will be found
Safe and sound
At peace
You win

Take It Slow

We don't know it all
We have flaws
Into existence you can speak
But love takes more than a week
To positively manifest
To be blessed
For goodness sake
Real work it takes
In days of time
We come to find
Little tell tell signs
And after all
This is something
You may not call
In the long run love
It's better to act like you know
And call it what it is
As to each other enjoyment
You give
And each day you live
Going with the flow
So take it slow

Dysfunction

On not so long ago
A friend reminded me
We all have skeletons
In our closet
To some lesser or greater degree
And sometimes in present day
They utterly show
We try to keep it down low
But unfortunately
Occasionally
In a fashion so hideously
They rear their head
Yet behaviors
Not all rooted in their past
Are hard to shed
Issues
Miscues
Disconnects
Abuse
One way or another
Are a part of us
All that are around suffer
But deal with it then best they can
With treatment it can be alleviated
But memories of what took place
Or what occurs now
Is sadly dysfunction

Relationship

A booty call
Has no appeal to me
Consensual
Casual sex
Continuously
Is not all
It's made out to be
Just meeting a physical need
Although pleasurable
It's hardly measurable
Needs emotional
Aren't tended too
After making time
What is next to do
Can we be devotional
Or is that too hard to do
When it comes down to it
In our heart of hearts
Can we draw the line
To stop living like this
It's no way to exist
Really only emptiness
When you can get a wholehearted
for real lifelong commitment
Worthy of you
With the idea one
That God has sent
The one that's meant
Can't miss
In a relationship

Pray... Don't Faint... Believe

Pray don't faint... Believe
Pray don't faint... Receive
God is faithful... Fully capable
To heal the land... Turn from
every wicked way
Pray don't faint... Believe
Pray don't faint... Receive
Nothing's impossible
His power is unstoppable
Have hope... Don't give up now
Stand
Pray till change comes
Pray until something happens
Pray till the victory is won
Pray don't faint ... Believe
Pray don't faint... Receive
Not a man that He can lie
He will make a way of escape for you and I
Pray don't faint... Believe

Go With God

None can be compared to Him
With Him you only win
His love goes beyond explaining
Automatically His love It's easy to be obtaining
We have His love forevermore to the end
No shadow of turning toward us
He perfects all concerning us
But God we must learn to trust
Pivotal now in this end time
It's absolutely a must
He goes Before us and
makes every crooked road straight
We must exercise our faith
Because He is able and steadfast
Never leaving nor forsaking us
But to higher heights taking us
Molding and making us
But we must not complain
But quiet remain
And His will maintain
For all is well and never in vain
It may be some rough patches
And storms of rain
But God is with you and me
So entirely blessed we can be
Kept in perfect peace
I can praise God in spite of what is going on
When all seems wrong
But as sure as the morning dawn
The God to whom I belong will give breakthrough
His promises yes and amen manifested
Grace and Mercy prevails
No good thing from God was withheld
His compassion overwhelmed

And loving kindness excelled
All His ways are true
You don't have to be moved
Stay with God
And go from Glory to Glory
The author and finisher of our story
You win and don't lose
The first and last
The Holy one
Which none surpass
The only wise God
Who is Most High
Choose
Let it be understood
He is the only God that is good
Go with God

Lost And, Turned Out

Established
Self sufficient
Enjoying life
Thriving
Not just surviving
Marvelous
In twentieth century
Society
In Tulsa
They were doing
Very fine
With their very own hospitals
And independent bus line
Their own businesses by the scores
On a grand scale
But the white folk
Said someone from there
Did something out of line
A heinous crime
Against a white citizen
False accusation
Then a standoff took place
A black man vowed to protect
Gunfire from his rifle shot
In retaliation
A mob and the klan ensued
A massacre followed
Hundreds of black people killed
And now what was once enterprising
Was now reduced to rubble
Devastation
Lost and turned out
From what they had attained
More than fifteen minutes of fame

It was a horrible shame
An absolute undeniable pain
How dare you try to overtake
Or a mecca independent make
Your dollars will I no longer forsake
Tulsa
Black Wall Street
1921
Lost and turned out

They Go On

They grimace
In pain
Which is excruciating
Trying to maintain
The sun shines
But internally
There isn't any warming
Longing for
A resemblance to normalcy
A multitude of ailments
Have them thinking
What is the use
Is my living entirely in vain
not feeling well
They are young
Only nearing fifty
It is hell
An existence limiting
Physical
Mental
Disabilities
To family and friends
Cause one to be somewhat
Of a liability
But they go on
Mostly because they have responsibilities
And challenges formidable
Real
They can't get the services and support they need
So many hold ups and breakdowns
Plainly and profoundly the system
Isn't helping the way they should
Cold and forbidding
Unforgiving

Struggling in the meantime
It is a mean time
So unkind
They must persevere
To live
In order not to die
The rain is falling
Yet they must navigate the weather
Inclement and ongoing
Putting on a good face
For what a soul is facing
However debasing
They need help
Like yesterday so many times
But somehow they go on
They survive
They say God's in control
Barely hanging on in the midst
But they remain fixed on mortality
Even if it isn't with the vigor and vitality
They once had
That is their reality
But they go on

Are You Ready For This

After four hundred years
Of being enslaved
We are liberated
We have endured
We have survived
Our legacy lingers
Resilient
Remarkable
Amazing
Even though racism
Has reared its hideous head
With a vengeance
We will still overcome
Bound for a destiny
That is so much more
We are on an unstoppable quest
Still we press
Making a way somehow
Look at how much time
We have in
By God's grace
We are still here
So mount up
To lay claim to
Unity
Solidarity
Harmony
We shall behold
Freedom
For which we have bled
Second class citizenship
A crock we've been hand fed
A crack we can no longer maintain
Putting into our veins

We must not kill us
And God we must trust
For our journey which ensues
Straighten up for what we are due
Prosperity stored up by the wicked
Is laid up for the just
So see how you're living
Cause reparations the Lord is giving
We must be found without spot
Or any wrinkle
To be eligible for a miracle
This has been centuries in the making
Repent to be partaking
For us God surely is not forsaking
If truly transparent
And your love for God is apparent
You will see what treasure awaits
At the end of the road
A gift of gold you cannot afford to miss
So the advesary resist
And be in position
To receive
In God believe
Are you ready for this

I Still Love You

I can't behave unseemly
I've got to be on one accord
Obey the Almighty
Moving forward
We may disagree
But let us agree to do so
Differences we may see
But I with love will still flow
I still love you
Even though I don't care for the things
you do
I'll be praying for you
We may be enemies
Opposing each other
But still my love
I will let you discover
Even from a distance
I will not let you suffer
Show you no resistance
Because love always
Is ultimately bigger
Than anything unlike it displayed
But I choose still to be compliant
Because at Calvary a statement was made
Love personified
Christ died
Selflessly
For you and I
So who am I
To love not to subscribe
I cannot defy this
The opportunity miss
Although we may not embrace
I still love you

Clothe Yourself

Social media
Is your platform
Where you showcase
Your goods
Scantily dressed
For all the world to see
Some of you are bold
You think it ok to expose
What God gave for eyes to behold
Sacred possession
Conceal it from humanity
It's fine to be sexy
However modestly
But with your husband
 in private
On the marriage bed only
I know some of you are lonely
Perhaps some are desperate
But for your bodies have some self respect
Clothe Yourself

Dark Skin

So beautiful indeed
From God
It's a masterpiece
Not a mistake but brilliant
A centerpiece
Comely and unique
Is the mystique
Dark chocolate
Pure and sweet
Full of melanin
Not melancholy
Oh what goodness
Prevails
And is to be exalted
Not to find fault in
A flawless design
A fixture
just what God had in mind
The moon and stars
 It does outshine
It is remarkable
And not an oddity
Valid
God spun this vibrant reality
The work of His hands
Dark skin

I Miss You

I miss you
I miss us
But you had enough
Misery
To last a lifetime
Sickness
Took a toll
And left an imprint
On my soul
But I miss you
To have a love
It's essence
Was so sweet
You were the kindest
Person
With compassion
You reached out
To overflowing
To so many
I was your spouse
And I loved you
But you have a lasting impression
On me too
What did I do to deserve you
I miss you
I want to kiss you
But you are with God now
And that's the best thing
No more pain
No more living in vain
No more rain
To deluge you
To ravage your body
But there's solace

But you are the one woman
I have truly loved
You are so blessed
You were my friend
The very best
And I miss you

Fixed

Watching the news
Can make you informed
But too many views
Of information
Can make you forget
Your first love
Remain steady
Cause this world's shaky
Maintain your gaze
Focus please
Stay locked in
Engaged
Admidst the world's going ons
Still have perfect peace
Do not marvel at this
But only believe
The report of the Lord
With everlasting eyes
Remain fixed

Angry Son

Sometimes
I want to cuss you out
You drank
You cheated
On my mother
But I never
Had the opportunity
To tell you
How I really felt
I am mad
And I have a right
Because you left us
Mom and my siblings
I was twelve
I really had no role model
My brothers had their pursuits
I was a pre teen
And was deserted
I got the short end of the stick
You served in the Navy
Before I was even conceived
And those two revere you
They got the same ill treatment from you
Yet it's so crazy
I still believe in the idea of family
I am advanced in age now
I am releasing you to God now
I suppose He will give me closure somehow
Meanwhile I forgive you
Because I'm supposed to
I don't love you
With a love that is family related
Cause you were never there
You were never familiar

But God is love
And I have got to love you
I can longer be
An angry son

This Simple Thing

A simple thing
An ordinary task
I thought with us
Integrity
Was in place
I thought it wasn't too much
To ask
I thought
We were in a space
That was safe
But it seems likely
You will not able to deliver
On a simple request
I thought
From the onset
We had good rapport
After all we are working
Toward a common goal
But because you uttered
From your mouth
On which
You didn't follow through with
Can we ever be whole
Can I really be with and trust you
I just want to comprehend
If good faith you can extend
Will you be legitimate
Or will I be unfortunately
With regret
When I felt for each other
We had respect
There has been perhaps
A simple case of neglect
And disregard

Or you just forgot
I will give you that
I hope we can correct
This misunderstanding
That it doesn't have a lasting effect
What can I expect
When you promised me
This simple thing

Separate

I don't know how
To really care for you
Except to buy you chips
I wish I could break through
I have never really been able to
Even though everyday
I am in your midst
I know it is what God wants
To somehow for us to unite
Have I failed
I know you have seen death first hand
With Mom and Clay going in your very arms
And this your soul haunts
But all of this harkens back
You have never had the knack
That you were never under attack
I don't know what happened to you
What in the past and in the present
Has captured you
But I haven't done anything harsh to you
For love to never be felt from you
Life is much too short
But you are stuck in a time warp
There are many issues unresolved
I can love you from a distance
I suppose with unemotional ties
We argue but I have stopped now
I guess I will never be able to reach you
And get you some much needed attention
But love up close I mean everyday affection
I don't believe we will ever encounter
I don't fit in your niche
Should I even bother
I don't think so

I have tried for more than two years
Since we have lived together
You are no better
I am not either
I am sorry
But I am kinda blue
The real you I never knew
You sit and stew
On the easy chair
I only say easy
Because you choose this easy existence
Where you don't have to try
You are incapable of doing so
But I will be out of your way soon
As soon as I can
I am on the verge of tears
Cause it's all quite sad
And all too real
However I can't bring myself to any
God help me not to be bitter and cold
But you can only go so far
Loving from a remote place
You are unable of change
Except God helps you
I have prayed for it
But it hasn't surfaced yet
You need your space
And I need mine too
In order to thrive
Maybe we have to be separate

I Love You

I love you
That is why
I'm trying to tell you
That some
Oh what you do
Is contrary
With what
The Almighty
Would have you to do
He doesn't
Want you to perish
Because
You're soul
He does cherish
I love you
So I try to
Breakthrough
Telling you
Despite
All that you do
God loves you
He has
Never
Stopped
Loving you
But first
You must come
To the truth
And makes Jesus
Your very own
Please
Accept salvation
I love you
Because you are

His creation
Why must you disown
And disobey
The very God
That gave you life
And formed you
In a special way
Into His image
Your sin gets
In His way
I love you
Your worth
Do not diminish
Don't with God
Be finished
He can transform
Having a wealth of compassion
He is waiting
To forgive you
Restore
And renew
He loves you
I do too
I cannot fail you
That is why I tell you
Because
He loves your soul
Give your intentional behavior
To a savior
Who does not hate you
Again He waits for you
Turn to Him
So He can live
Immeasurably
In your heart
A light that outshines

The darkness
Yes I tell you
This He wants to impart
That is why
I've tried to tell you
The way you were going is a dead end
A freefall to hell
This is the truth
Spoken in love
Because you are worth it
And not worthless
This is why I tell you
Jesus to pursue
Accept eternal salvation
Deny eternal damnation
And yes this pertains to you
You may have never knew
This is why I tell you
Because
I love you

No More Masks

You know what God loves?
That is... the truth
We have had so much turmoil
A stench in our nostrils
That has spoiled
Far too long
Unjust treatment
As ancestors
Sung spirituals
In the fields
They would yield
Their dignity
But now it's time out
From this charade
What are we
Fools
No no no
For generations
We have played
By your twisted rules
Now it's time
A turning point
No more modern day
Slavery
With destinies
You will no longer take
Indecent liberties
In every way
We will be free
 We have done your tasks
And chores
And washed
Your dirty drawers
Our resolve is stronger

WARERESOURCES AND PUBLISHING

WE ARE AN ALL IN ONE,

ONE STOP PUBLISHING COMPANY!!!!

W.R.P. is a modest but skillful and knowledgeable Christian Publishing Company. We specialize in getting authors into print. We embrace and guide each author like a member of our family. We treat you fairly and recognize the importance of building a lasting relationship with you as an author. Join us in the walk to promote prosperity along with the message of encouragement and peace. Be one of the authors we transform and prepare for the world of information and books.

FEEL FREE TO CONTACT US@
www.wareresources.com

1-888-469-4850 EXT. 2

http://www.facebook.com/pages/Ware-Resources-and-Publishing

www.ingramcontent.com/pod-product-compliance
Lightning Source LLC
Chambersburg PA
CBHW062147100526
44589CB00014B/1718